First published in Great Britain in 2001 by
POETRY NOW
Remus House,
Coltsfoot Drive,
Peterborough, PE2 9JX
Telephone (01733) 898101
Fax (01733) 313524

Copyright Contributors 2001

HB ISBN 0 75432 614 4
SB ISBN 0 75432 615 2

FOREWORD

Although we are a nation of poets we are accused of not reading poetry, or buying poetry books. After many years of listening to the incessant gripes of poetry publishers, I can only assume that the books they publish, in general, are books that most people do not want to read.

Poetry should not be obscure, introverted, and as cryptic as a crossword puzzle: it is the poet's duty to reach out and embrace the world.

The world owes the poet nothing and we should not be expected to dig and delve into a rambling discourse searching for some inner meaning.

The reason we write poetry (and almost all of us do) is because we want to communicate: an ideal; an idea; or a specific feeling.

Poetry is as essential in communication, as a letter; a radio; a telephone, and the main criterion for selecting the poems in this anthology is very simple: they communicate.

CONTENTS

DAWN MIST WALTZ

Placid sits the river
As dawn mist waltzes
Through the trees
And bids them be
Angels for the early eye to see

Through tight grass
Gossip slowly slides
With tales of roses on the rise
That comes as no surprise
To the moles who earthly sigh

Fresh petals retch
As the old set sail
Across the void of mist
Like an ancient forgotten wish
That makes the ripples twist

Now time has moved along
And trees are only trees
And the river turns and runs
Toward the warmth of sun
That nightmares always shun

A E S Gamage

ANDALUSIA

When springtime's promise is not kept
And hopes for summer very slight,
I feel drawn to a sun-filled land
As moths are drawn to candlelight.

There clear skies resent the clouds
And give them room reluctantly,
Preferring vapours small and white
To masses black and thundery.

Caught in the sun's intense heat,
The landscape trembles in the mist,
Changing perceptions so we see
Towers that tilt and trees that twist.

Cooings come softly on the breeze,
With drowsy twitters interspersed,
A chorus of specific sounds
From woodland choirs well-rehearsed.

There flowers have a richer glow,
More vibrant in the dazzling light.
Dipped in nature's opulent dyes,
They seem to blossom overnight.

Hanging gardens on every street,
Trailing garlands on whitewashed walls,
Celebrate their living colour
And mourn each petal as it falls.

I will walk through palatial halls
Where silk-robed sultans once held sway.
I'll see the splendours that they saw
And dream their dreams of yesterday.

Celia G Thomas

LONDON TOWN

The cockney accent is the best of all
Come down here China and have a ball
Bring wiv ya your trouble and strife
Feast your mince pies and see some life
Come on a bus or in your own jam jar
Together me old mate, we'll visit a bar
If ya like we'll go to Petticoat Lane
Where no two stalls are the same
Or we can go down the Old Kent Road
In the rub-a-dub, of beers we'll have a load
I'll teach you how cockney ya can talk
While we do the famous Lambeth Walk
We could take a stroll to Downing Street
Or go to the tower, if you can manage it on your tired
plates of meat.
Ya'll agree London's the best place you've seen
Living in Buck Palace is the Queen
And as she parades wearing her crown
Like us, she loves London Town.

Graeme Doherty

Unity's Dream

Hearts lament thine euphoria for living,
So free to prosper 'neath tender moon,
Caring, sharing, loving and forgiving,
Concurrence of understanding not seen too soon,
Voices collaborate as with angels sing,
Replenishment ascend as the new morn sun,
Wash cynicism asunder amid life's crystal spring
As hearts combine afore day is done.

Chilled wind of illusion flee to pass,
Upon the morrow shalt morality comply,
Luscious be our dream clear as glass,
Prosperity's embrace ne'er to deny,
Harmonious rapture 'tween a tender vow,
Foretell thy destiny o wanton heart,
Aloft meadows burnished 'neath heaven bow,
Unity's tender dream now to us impart.

Steve Kettlewell

MOONBEAMS

It's two in the morning, I really can't sleep,
Crawled out of my bed, through the curtain to peep,
The moon in the sky cast a heavenly glow,
Everybody asleep, just for me was the show,
I slipped on my clothes, crept out through the door,
Popped on my boots, left slippers on floor,
Up into the meadow, it were if it were day,
Onto my right there were fox cubs at play,
All the nocturnals were out and about,
Bats chattering messages, no need to shout,
Did I hear music down there in the glen?
Bodhrans and fiddles echoed again,
Moonbeams reflected on silvery streams,
Like prisms and rainbows, how brightly they gleam,
Creeping on slowly I peeped 'round a rock,
Saw leprechauns dance underneath a big crock,
As the moon disappeared beneath a grey cloud,
I awoke to a bell ring - 7-30 quite loud.

W Curran

NATURE'S TRANSFORMATIONS

Sorting through the stones,
Finding mans' rubbish left behind.
But nature has the answer,
Glass rubbed smooth with a frosted design.

Everything with jagged edges,
Rubbed smooth with the incoming tide.
With the sand littered with objects,
Excitement for treasures will not subside.

Nature transforms mans' structures,
To bring back beauty where we lack.
Coats it with love and beauty,
For man has lost his tack!

Even mans' creative landscapes,
Can't beat natures' rugged design.
For in those crooks and crannies,
You'll find secrets and treasurers to define!

The shoreline is an ever-moving picture,
For life keeps moving on.
Man keeps on with his destruction,
While nature had no war to be won!

Ann Beard

BITTER-SWEET NIGHT

Arm in arm we walked that night
So very much in tune
Wishing we had the rest of time
To walk beneath the moon
The hours were passing quickly by
We didn't want the day
To creep upon our precious dreams
And take them all away

We later lay down side by side
What comfort there we found
Our bodies still - the beating of
Our hearts the only sound
We soon embraced and gently kissed
Our bodies now aglow
Exploring all the sensuous joys
That only lovers know

Our hands caressed our eager limbs
With gentle, loving care
Responsive senses sprang to life
At joy we knew we'd share
An all-consuming power became
The true reality
As then I gave myself to you
So very willingly

We slept contented, close and warm
Though deep within each heart
An aching dread was waiting for
The time we had to part
You left me, dear, tears in your eyes
And I was crying too
Now memory's all we have until
I once again hold you

Peggy Matthews

THE SHEPHERD

Be not afraid in life sublime
Use hope as wings and merrily climb.
When the will of flesh is weak
My voice in spirit shall speak,
There is nothing that is yours but Mine.

I am the flame of suns so bright
I am the shepherd of starry night;
I am the guest and host
The watcher at the post,
I am your love and you are My light.

If you but give yourself to Me
Not in doubt but wholeheartedly;
Your open prayers I shall heed
When you call to Me in need,
You are a wave and I the endless sea.

All things come true if you believe.

Nick Purchase

BABYDOLL

Beetles battle out their blues.
Boys will win and boys will lose.
Glory gains a sandy fort.
Busting beauties shall be bought.

Lionesses land and lie.
Beauty sits behind their eyes.
Open sky lets go, breaks down.
Corpses rest on shadowed ground.

Sunlight combs a grieving gift.
From the floor, her lashes lift.
Setting on a weaker soul.
Dolls will dice and death will toll.

Alexa Konik

MY FUN BOX

I've got a box with clowns in all so bright,
I have been saving them up all right.
I love their big round noses,
Also their cheers like dark pink roses.
Their baggy pants all covered with patches
Of colours all stitched around,
It must be great to be a clown.
Yellow hair some have got,
But some wear hats with flowers on top,
Such big grins they have upon their faces so wide,
They give me fun tears in my eyes.
I love my clowns they are a funny lot,
Many days I sit down and take them from their box.
Some have long feet, also tight-fitted coats,
But I've got one I love the most.
I call him 'Mr Rags' so scruffed is he,
At times I take him from the box
And take him out with me.

Marion Staddon

MEET ME IN THE GREENWOOD

Meet me, my princess, when awakens the dawn,
Down in the greenwood where our true love was born,
Where we skipped o'er the sward with the warm, summer breeze
And frolicked amongst oak and sycamore trees.

Meet me, your servant, when the light of day breaks
For to soothe my poor heart which, without you, doth ache,
In that small, secret clearing where the red deer belong
And the blackbird and mistle thrush sing their morning song.

Meet me in the greenwood when the rising sun shines,
Where we shared a brief moment with our bodies entwined,
And we'll dance once again in that magical place,
Barefoot and breathless in a loving embrace.

A R Hawthorn

A SUMMER LAMENT

Dear Philomena, sweet muse of the world,
at the sound of whose voice
my heart is unfurled,
why does it always so happen to me
that after each meeting I glisten with glee?

Dear charming mole by the side of your face,
lending enchantment and favour and grace,
finely-cut countenance turning to me
courtesy words without hands to agree.

O for a sprig of your blossoming heart!
A loan of your fingers might bear me a part.
But rarely, if ever, your stern eye unbends.
Devil may care while we stay loving friends.

George Pearson

SAY CHEESE

We're a happy bunch at 42,
Bringing smiles to all of you.
Catching moments, large and small,
And we'll send you a card, if you don't call.

From holidays to weddings, we'll see you right,
And care for your photos, far into the night.
Our 'mini lab', is second to none,
With hours, and overnights all quickly done.

We'll share your tears, and laughter too,
It's our pleasure to help, every day through.
But, please remember, when tempers are fraught,
Good manners cost nothing, or so we are taught.

We'll always try to do our best,
Even lost photos, we'll make them our quest.
Rainy days, and sunny smiles,
Photos taken from across the miles.
But when things go wrong, it's up to us,
We'll sort your problem, with simply no fuss.

Janice Thorogood

JOY IS STRENGTH

I write a poem every day
To tell this world so dull and grey
Dress in the colours that beautify life
Ease away from the pains of strife
Looking to quality in many smiles
You'll find the means to travel miles,
Take for instance baby boys in blue
Men of the future who'll care for you
And little girls so gentle and serene
They'll bless you with love and answer a dream
Look to tomorrow when their journey is bound
To learn of wisdom and its peaceful sound
Let our strength be their provision for life
And our joy's *their* overcoming any bitter knife.

Linda Daly

PRIDE AND PREJUDICE

When people meet
Their hands extend
Delighted to greet
A prospective friend.

When white meets black
Where is this token?
A shaking of hands
Is a barrier broken.

A stare or evasion
Is a barrier made,
The foundation stone
Of a wall is laid.

The dividing wall grows,
Dark one side, pallid the other,
A contrasting shame
Of brother for brother.

Ann Hulme

MOMENTS IN RHYME

Moments in rhyme, are magical to me,
they set my tortured, twisted mind free.
It's like an unstoppable, never-ending flow,
putting smiles on faces, making cheeks glow.

Sense, nonsense, humour, seriousness,
laughing at his highness' imperiousness.
As he eats his breakfast, with silver spoon,
after a heavy night out, barking at the moon.

Deludedly believing, he's the lord of the manor,
supremely unaware, he's just short of a tanner.
Left in his silk pocket, because I've spent it all,
My name's Millicent, I'm the queen of the ball.

Down at the dance hall, every single weekend,
half his net income, my intention to spend.
Well, he did marry me for better or worse,
though I doubt if I'll show him,
my cute little verse!

Millicent Coleman

THE JOY OF CHRISTMAS

Each passing year our hearts will leap once more
In wonder at the far-off, lowly birth
Of him, behind a stable's creaking door,
Who, destined to endure the grief on Earth
Which mean, malicious men did on him pour,
Was born to suffer pain and anguish sore.

Rejoicing with this Christ whom we adore -
God's gift to us of timeless, priceless worth -
Forget for now the cross he later bore
And celebrate with glad and joyous mirth.
Remembering the poor just as before,
Be merry and let all your spirits soar.

Keith Ellel

PASSING TIME

Passing the time, mind on idle,
to the computer, I quietly sidle.
Sit gently down upon the seat,
to see what creations I'll meet.

That's the thing about writing,
it's so incredibly exciting.
To sit with computerised pen,
with nothing, but suddenly then.

Creation! Originality! Invention!
I'm writing about things,
I had no intention.

Flowing from the mind,
into waiting fingers.
Literature, helping pass time,
which otherwise lingers.

Andy Monnacle

WRITING POETRY

Put your trust in poets
They won't tell you any lies.
There's no furtive behaviour,
No hidden agenda or spies.

We try to be so honest
As transparent as can be.
You won't get sly, dry glances
From the likes of Yeats or me.

Words should point to perfect truths
Or why use them at all?
Wasting time in politics
Can lead to rise, then fall.

Take words to the waiting crowd,
Listen who gather there.
You won't hear better wisdom
In a month or in a year.

Scatter in the air waves,
Harangue the doughty press,
Spit or swirl your wonder words,
Don't let their meaning rest.

Weave and write and speechify,
Dance your words around.
Order them and line them up,
Just listen to their sound.

Now my poem's written
And the words have broken loose.
They're running free upon the page
Invigorating their use.

Keith Melbourne

REBIRTH
(Dedicated to my special parents)

You gave me hope when all was gone,
You gave me love when I'd had none,
You gave your smile when I was sad,
Then dried my tears till I was glad.

You rescued me from my unknown fate -
God knows how long you had to wait?

But now I want so much to say,
Whilst thinking of that special day,
The day you took me on your knee
And I became my real 'me'.

So Mum and Dad, let my message be:
'Thank you both for adopting me!'

Clare Cork

RECYCLED

Parched the earth without its touch,
That falls on soil and breathes out life,
That fuels food from leaf to root,
And on its way to the river bed,
Runs the river to its end,
To merge with lake and on again,
Flowing stream is on its way,
Towards the sea and destiny,
Gathered up by sun to sphere,
Rekindled in the atmosphere,
Comes to earth again in storm,
In cloudburst rage, in flake, in hail,
Never seen in summer months,
And winter, sheer superfluous.

Hugh Jackson

SMOKING

I see the smoke come from your lips
And then you blow blue rings
And I think that you are clever
When I see you do those things

But when I hear you coughing
And you sound like you might choke
I wonder why you spend your money
Just to have a smoke

Now I know it may be trendy
And your friends they do it too
But have you really thought about
What cigarettes can do

They can make your life a misery
They can shorten it as well
They can make you most unhealthy
And make your life a living hell

So although I think you're clever
Blowing smoke rings like you do
I would rather stay more healthy
Than gamble with my life like you

J A Jenkins

AN ARCHER I WOULD BE

In Cambridge where I used to live
I got bored and thought I'd give
Some time on something I might like
Perhaps on climbing or a hike.
Then, in a field nearby
Saw targets and some arrows fly
Shot by fellows dressed in green
With such a tunic I could preen.
An archer then, I thought I'd be
And joined the proper club you see.
They showed me how to hold the bow,
To fit the arrow and let go,
How to aim and how to score,
They said they could not show me more,
I toed the line and eyed the gold,
Tried to remember what I'd been told,
Drew back the string and then let loose,
Turned bright red, felt like a goose.
I nowhere near the target put,
The arrow landed near my foot,
Ambitions to be Robin Hood
Flew from my mind, I wished I could
Disappear from the field
And so, the bow I did yield,
I very quietly stole away
To never again with archers play

Harry Gill

EASTER HOPE

Christ be my guide as I follow His way.
Faith be my guard in sickness and health,
Truth in my heart from morning till night,
Trust in the Spirit all through the day.
God take my mind; let prayer be my wealth.
In living and dying let Christ be my light.

Christ guide my feet every step of the way,
God in my mind, His love in my heart.
Mercy my hope, His Word I must find.
Christ guide my thought whenever I pray.
God keep my hands in goodness apart.
Thanks be to God for His love of mankind.

Christ in my thought on the day of His death,
Jesus beside me in the journey of life,
Hope in my heart at His rising today,
Love in my being at each intake of breath,
Peace with me now and the end of all strife
When Christ is my guide as I follow His way.

Uvedale Tristram

BOUNTY HUNTER

Much have I travelled in the realms of gold,
but not made any,
essayed in countries hot, dry, wet or cold
to earn an honest penny,
but not earned many.

A pilgrim, but no puritan, I crossed
the Atlantic, to take stock and look
around. Thanksgiving. America is where I lost
some dollars to a pious crook
but garnered a little wisdom from a book.

I followed the Conquistadors from Spain
to Eldorado, but my treasure trove
was immaterial and I came home again,
enriched only by pleasure
and experience in equal measure.

Trailed Moschos and Alexander around the Med.
The eastern Levant
drove notions of abundance from my head,
all dreams of conquest. Scant
is the sum of such as I possess, or need or want.

Tracked Marco Polo to the orient,
Conrad and Doubting Thomas,
saw all the places where Magellan went,
each filled with promise
of reward at journey's end, and that's where home is.

The fire burns brightly, red cinders glowing.
Outside, dark night. Here, in my treasury, with pad
and pen at hand, and recollection throwing
continents across my inner eye, I calculate the bounty that I've had.
Gloating like Shylock, I add and add and add.

Norman Bissett

ITALY

Vineyards, orchards melt away,
Blend into the mountains.
Dusky villas, shadows fall,
Hiding secret fountains.

Athalia Pyzer

PROLOGUE TO WHITBY LIFEBOAT

Courage does not blossom as we grow
nor is transmitted as a heated glow
but is born to all of womankind
though we may never feel or know.

Courage is not transcribed to fit the mange
one cannot place, remove, or rearrange
but manifests itself at some unscripted need
enables common man some fate to change.

Courage, like God, is everywhere we are
it dwells within, though distant, oft afar
and if for some 'tis thankfully remote
from few it beams like some unclouded star.

E Langford

THE CRYSTAL RIVER

Oh in the morning,
Give me warning, what you need,
I know you want my speed, for you.
I take every moment,
All the things that you can see,
Down to meet the rolling sea, you know.

Create in the sunshine,
All the power that people need,
Their factories to feed, you know,
Trees to the basin,
Where the mills are growing fast,
Take away the fields of grass from me.

Call my name the crystal river,
Running down forever away from you,
Say goodbye you rocky mountains,
Crystal fountains, away from you.

You take all my life blood,
And then put nothing back,
My banks they start to crack and die,
Sun takes its toll now,
No more time to help you live,
I gave all I could give, and free.

Wait till the morning,
The rain may come again,
Washing power into my veins once more.
Turn then full circle,
We wait for nothing more,
The tide has turned to shore again.

John Cook

MY MOON NYMPH

With wide-eyed wonder, I see
Such a dream before me
As the moon casts its silver light
I can hardly believe what's in my sight.

She is sitting on a lily pad,
Her little face looks so sad.
'Pray little one, what's wrong?'
Her reply is, 'I've lost my song.

Without my song what use am I?'
Then she flies off, with no goodbye.
The following night I do return,
To see what else I can learn.

My moon nymph is sitting on the ground
I can hear this magical sound.
The little one has found her voice
She tells me she had to make a choice.

At first I do not understand
Until I watch her walk away, on land.
She turns, and waves goodbye to me
Her lovely smile a joy to see.

Jeanette Jackson

THE ODEON

I remember watching movies
At the Odeon on Leeds
Wit friends who were the soundtrack
Of my spiritual needs,
And in that picture palace
Of the sixties I began
To witness the perfection
That was idolised by Man.

I remember smoking freely
In the darkness of my dreams
As movie stars compounded
My belief in many schemes,
And in the crowded silence
I could feel serenity
Encroach upon my thinking
For the film's entirety.

I remember each performance
On the massive silver screen
That energised emotions
With each scintillating scene,
And there were many lovers
Melting into works of art
Inside the heaving presence
Of a city's pulsing heart.

I remember how those movies
Left me feeling unconfined
And seemingly uplifted
In my overburdened mind,
But in the neon chaos
Life's reality kicked in
Amid the roaring traffic
And the crowd's incessant din.

Iaian W Wade

MY DEAREST DEAR

My dearest dear - save me a dream,
that in a moment it will seem -
love is drifting thro' the night
as dreams entwine - tho' not in sight.

To feel the softness of your hand,
in this enchantment we do stand -
when you gently touch my cheek
I hear those words we need not speak.

As a sigh from the sky above,
softly comes the warmth of love -
A fleeting glance that's so serene
my dearest dear - save me a dream.

Jon Arden

THE SALES

It's amazing when you stop and think,
Of the sales they hold each season,
They really must be doing well,
Of course . . . if that's the reason!

One week it's special offers and drinks,
And twenty per cent off shoes,
The next, it's ten off coloured reds,
And then it's twelve off blues.

I see they have a winter sale,
That makes the customers sing,
Trouble is, in just two weeks,
They hold one for spring.

Then after that they have mid-season,
And then any other silly reason,
I am sure they pray, 'these gimmicks won't fail,'
'Cause after that it's the summer sale.

The summer's gone, now autumn's here,
Let's have a sale for customer cheer,
I know it won't be very long,
Before it's end of season song.

Which goes with discounts on the separates,
Plus winter coats with great big epaulets,
And big strong boots made for the snow,
Look at the date, you'd never know,
Once again we have . . . Christmas here,
'When do you start the sale my dear?'

J Deekes

WAR

I hear airplanes flying way up high.
They are dropping missiles from the sky.
A tear of sadness falls from my eye,
As I think to myself - this is no way to die.

Helen Riley

THE OTHER MAN'S GRASS

My husband said, 'It's time we went
Upon this house enough we've spent.
Let's find a place that is brand new
With far less work for me and you.'

The agents came up with a find,
It was enough to blow my mind.
Brand sparkling new from door to door.
'Well, really, could we ask for more?'

The day we moved it poured with rain.
Had someone mentioned the flood plain?
The garden was a sea of mud,
But surely it would never flood.

For days and days it rained non-stop
The pond was full up to the top,
And when it rained still more and more
The water crept beneath the door.

The brand new carpets were a mess,
My husband's comments you have guessed.
The other house was very old
But always dry and never cold.

It doesn't always make much sense
To look beyond the garden fence.
The greenest grass you'll ever find
Is often growing there inside.

I M Morison

CAMPFIRE NIGHT

In the winter night hour chill
The air around is cold and still
Sound is muffled by the snow
Shining orange in the campfire glow

Songs are sung to pass the night
A minstrel plays to give delight
A wandering dancer, monk and more
Sagas told of days of yore

As fathers now and their fathers before
They speak of hunters' deeds with awe
And huddling from that winter cold
They marvelled at those days of old

Wrapped in cloaks still cold and damp
They gathered in this winter camp
Patient, waiting for signs that bring
The coming of the warmth of spring.

Ray Ryan

TIME FOR A RHYME

It's grand to see poets returning to rhyme
Perhaps now some will be treasured for a long, long time.
Some of the bards of long ago,
Must be so pleased to see poetic lines flow.
There is an art in composing rhyme.
Once it is mastered it stays with you for all time.
And it stays around for many to treasure
For many to derive much pleasure.

Betty Green

MAYTIME MADNESS

On such a night that doth beguile,
Near woodland, I did rest awhile,
And watched as pixies passed in file,
All in the month of May.

I watched as though in mystic trance,
As they began their elfin dance,
Two steps retreating - then advance,
They trod their merry way.

Then suddenly, whilst in retreat,
They stilled their tiny prancing feet,
No more, the magic pulsing beat,
Or rhyming of the lay.

Lace gossamer all fell away,
As ended their sweet roundelay,
Then I awoke in bed I lay,
All in the month of May.

Arthur L Haskell

WINTER PALETTE

Tapestries of fields unfold,
Yellow ochre, green and gold,
Bright beneath a sunlit sky,
A v-shaped trail of geese glides by.

A river murmurs on its way,
Adding silver to the day,
Snowdrops mass beneath the trees,
Whispering softly in the breeze,
Signs of spring to rouse the heart,
Bidding winter's chill depart.

Joyce H Honeyman

POOR BEASTS

The lush grass is all *they* chew
Their skins are used for leather shoes
Their bones are melted down for glue
Those bones are fed to others too
Agriculture or a mad zoo?
As MAFF seemed lost without a clue
To burn or bury what to do?
As the disease goes raging through
How long before we hear a 'Moo!'
Poor beasts! What have we done to you?

John Smurthwaite

IS THAT THE TIME?

Is that the school bell church bell,
Clock in the hall?
Whichever it is
It tolls for us all.

You'd be late for lessons,
Wedding day vows,
The clock chimes late
Resulting in rows.

We live by a heartbeat,
The ticking clock,
Rallying around
Like sheep in a flock.

The heart and clock
Calling time runs down
What's happening . . .?
I've come unwound.

Ann Weavers

TICK TOCK

Tick tock, tick tock, tick tock,
Life passes by to the ticking of a clock.
When young, birthdays, school holidays
And Christmases never seem to come.
But when older all flash by
Merged into one
The 'new' pop song you've just heard
On the radio,
Was in reality in the 'charts' long ago.
When young you were told not to wish
Your life away, 'It'll happen one day'
And in your heart you know it's true,
As years later about missed chances you sit and rue.
Tick tock, tick tock, tick tock,
Your life is melting away with the ticking of a clock.
By every second, by every minute and by every hour,
The clock regulates time, over which you have no power.

Bardon 2001

YOU TOOK ME

Behind my tender eyes I don't reveal
The glowing passion that I feel
The heavy eyelids of truth and blame,
Touching the centre of the flame.
Shutting out the loneliness that I fear,
Showing my passion in form of a tear.

You took me out of the darkness
Where love is full of sorrow and mist,
And brought me into the brightness,
Where true love really exists.

I see the happiness across your face
Your expression of love takes me to a place,
Where the meaning of sadness is never known
But still I'm isolated on my own.
One word you say could have let me be,
Holding you whilst laying next to me.

You brought me into the light
Where everything is clear to see,
Knowing that my feelings for you are right,
But they can be even stronger if you're with me.

You are more to me than a fairground attraction,
You gave me love and satisfaction,
Your confidence and self esteem, I have to admire
So strong full of hope and desire.
Knowing your life from day to day,
I don't know if mine's worth to stay.

You took me into the brightness
Leaving behind the feeling of despair
Showing me the effect of loveliness,
And the real meaning of the word care.

Nayland Smith

NATURE'S BEAUTY

I walked my dog to the beach today
The trees looked fantastic on the way,
Autumn colours to be seen
Red and yellow, bronze and green.

The sea was crashing on the shore
Each wave gave a mighty roar,
Seagulls soared and flew around
Making their shrill and shrieking sound.

Glistening pearls of morning dew
Adorn the path along the way,
Shimmer with sunlight fresh and new
A beautiful start to another day.

We turn, the sea behind us now
Our home not very far away,
Starlings bathe in a gutter stream
While in the trees two squirrels play.

This route we've walked so many times
Beneath a canopy of trees,
Dropping their leaves of gold and red
A carpet soft on which to tread.

Beth Gardiner

MEADOW

Please meet these people who are a special three,
and just imagine the world they would see,
as these are people of a different kind.
For the first is a woman who is blind,
one who can't judge by colour or race,
but she can feel the warmth of the sun on her face,
she can smell the scent of each and every flower,
and can taste Nature's fruit, be it sweet or sour.
Yes, she knows she is blind,
but she leaves those thoughts behind,
for she is as happy as I am.
Next is the second who is a deaf man,
one who can't judge by speech or sound,
but under his feet he can feel the soft ground,
he can also feel the sun's warm glow,
and can see all the colours of the rainbow.
Yes, he knows he cannot hear,
but he leaves his conscience clear,
for he is happy and is not cruel.
Finally is the third who is a complete fool,
one who can't judge common or regal air,
but for Nature's things he does care,
he can wonder about the colours the rainbow does cast,
and can feel the warmth of the sun in his grasp.
Yes, we know that he does not understand,
but he is happy here in this meadowland.

(No matter what you face,
always try to greet it,
with a song in your heart,
and a smile upon your lips.)

Dale Mullock

DINING ON STYLE

At the table sat my guests,
All well groomed and all well dressed.
As the food was laid by a servant
Eyes widened and became very observant.

At the table prayers were said,
Thanks were given from the wine to the bread.
As dishes were passed around the table,
We all listened to Mrs Bishop's fable.

At the table mouths filled up,
Noises diminished to a chew and a sup.
Knives and forks danced for a while,
Followed by compliments with a satisfying smile.

At the table coffee was served.
Eyes became tired as tummies became curved.
Then coats were donned and my guests began to go.
I think that my new table stole the show!

Debra Neale

LIFE

Babies and children will never know
Of the world around them
Until they all grow,

Teenagers of the world today
Are still learning
New things every day.

Men and women think
They have learned with age
Still they argue, and fight with rage,

Old people tell us
'Be kind to all;
So what *have* we learned about life?

Actually, nothing at all.

Angie Stevens

A HORSE TRAINER

There is a horse trainer who is a man
who races his horses always on the sand
he is smart and supposedly kind
like a dustcart, not in mind

This particular trainer
raced a horse in a claimer
It won by a length
showing everyone its real strength

All racehorse trainers work hard all day
never really having much of a say
except with the owners and the few
but some would find that's not always true

There is a trainer who is a man
who likes to race horses on the sand
the horses gallop with all their might
to the finishing line and within sight

Kristina Howells

THERE CAN BE GOODNESS ACHIEVED FROM MONEY

An excess of money is not a good thing,
But happiness to some - I'm sure it could bring,
If it's used wisely and for a good cause -
When deciding to spend - a moment we pause,
Contemplate deeply, and make sure its use -
Is put to advantage - and not to abuse,
A small helping hand to friends we could give -
Assisting in making life easier to live,
Oh! What it would mean if I were that one-
All present selfishness within me gone.

Elizabeth Jones

DOWN, BLUE, SAD AND TRUE

So depressed, feeling down,
No longer a silly, happy clown,
But a sad and worried 16-year old,
Who's got a lot of problems, yet tries to be bold,
Who puts on a brave, dependent smile,
To everyone else, but it wears off after a while,
When all alone, with no one there,
No one to talk to, no one to care,
With domestics at home, she's so depressed,
And exams coming up, no wonder she's stressed,
She's got a lot on her plate, right now this lass,
And though she feels like slitting herself with glass,
She must realise that things will get better
But before they do, her tear-stained face must get wetter!

Tamzyn Dyson

A Sonnet To -

G roaning under this cumbersome baggage,
A rrival prompt at the air terminal.
T ravellers rush to weigh in their luggage,
W ithout which, problems will be minimal.
I nto queues for seats and boarding passes,
C rowds and cases are fast multiplying.
K isses goodbye from the milling masses,
A ttention to screens constantly flashing.
I n every spot, security intense.
R eceive our tickets, row 10, A, B, C,
P assport control, then we've cleared the last fence,
O ut in the lounge with time for a coffee.
R elax and wait for the call to depart,
T he holiday's off to a flying start!

Pat Heppel

MEDITATION

I wander along and my thoughts travel far.
Like a bird on the wing I would reach for a star.
Troubles and worries are left far behind
As my mind travels free I am no longer blind.
I pass over mountains so tall and serene,
And I spy the wild animals so seldom seen
For man has brought fear in his passage through life
To conquer the world he has filled it with strife.
I see the tall forests, silent and still,
Yet filled with creation only Nature can fill.
I learn to be humble, for little we know
Of the Great Spirit's plans for the future, and so
Let's open our minds, our ears and our eyes
For the lessons are there if we choose to be wise.

Kathleen Holmes

OUR HERITAGE

Poets can write of pastures green,
of Nature's beauty still unseen
by those whose eyes as yet can't see,
and take in such serenity.

One can describe an April day,
the burgeoning of buds in May;
It's difficult to educate
one unversed to appreciate.

How lucky is the one whose eyes
are opened to the bluest skies;
Who looks beyond clouds of white,
and soars above the birds in flight.

Some people go through life, it seems
seeing little, having few dreams;
Their life is poorer, because they
take in so little, on their way.

Perfection is not ours, but we
can see it in each leafy tree;
In dewy petals of a rose,
in every plant that Nature grows.

Hear it in the whispering breeze,
birdsong from hedgerows, and from trees;
Hear it in the lark's soaring song,
that seems to linger all day long.

These wonders everyone can share,
we only have to look, they're there;
Awaiting us, this golden age,
this lovely world, our heritage.

James Kimber

BIGGEST EVER BUMBLEBEE

In the middle of an ancient elephant tree,
sat the world's biggest ever bumblebee.
It had circumnavigated tempestuous seas,
to collect pollen from the gigantic flowers,
of the one and only, ancient elephant tree.

Flying from east to west, it had searched the land,
bulbously buzzing, crossing ice floes and sand.
On a quest for pollen, to sustain its humble life,
support its stricken mother, children and wife.

It buzzed everywhere, until one day espying,
the all-seeing bear, renowned for not lying.
Questioning the beast, about the elephant tree,
the bear replied, 'It appears at a quarter to three,
six days a week, south of the giant's pot of tea!'

And that, my friends, is how the world's biggest
ever bumblebee
Came to be sitting in the world's one and only
ancient elephant tree.

Mandy Ann Cole

A Short, Annoying Little Poem

I am a poem, that's if you didn't guess, that's what I am,
this is only the second line of this ode, since it began,
now starts the third line of this poem, or is it prose?
There may be a fourth one after the last, I sort of suppose,
if this verse doesn't make sense, or rhyme, that'll be fine,
it wouldn't make any difference, as this is the last line.

Christopher Higgins

HALLOWE'EN NIGHTS

Wind whistles down the churchyard drive
Spookily whispering sort of jive.
Ghostly haunting waves of chat
Whispering nerves scares on track.

Rattle of chains, fluttering of bats
Shuttle of the pester rats
Whining of howling, prying cats
Church clock strikes on the roof again
At the count of ten
As I fear I shall never do it again.

Something walks over my foot
Dripping blood Dracula or a cruel one-headed nave
Pictures in my mind stands far back am afraid
All silly devil eyes, all stare back
It's my childhood, silly mates laughing at
My mischief joke, I'll get you back another year.

A J Renyard

VANISHED DELIGHTS

So many things I can no longer do,
    Which over many years gave me such pleasure,
Now eyes and legs are failing, balance too;
    Things which one takes for granted, all one's days
    And bit by bit, unnoticed, melt in haze
And this and that no more engage one's leisure.

Long country walks, summer and winter taken,
    And cycle rides which much increased our scope.
The never-ending joys as blossoms waken
    As with our sketching group, we blithely painted
    Some well-known scene, as if but new acquainted,
Sometimes to fail, though never losing hope.

And further back, the thrill of country dance,
    Body and mind in perfect harmony
While music bade us 'sett', 'retreat', 'advance'.
    And party times with friends long since departed,
    Who, worries set aside, were happy hearted,
Who worked and talked and laughed and grew with me.

But if the joys of Heaven I attain
    And guardian angel kindly bids me tell
What earthly pleasure I would know again
    While learning with celestial life to cope,
    And greeting long-lost friends - I'd name my dearest hope -
To meet with all the cats I've loved who well,
And stroking silky fur, hear purring swell!

Kathleen M Hatton

I DID MY BEST

Some work to live
Some live to work
I never had a chance
In life or romance
Always under a cloud
Could cry out loud
Anyway what is life
A house, two kids, a wife?
They say love will blossom and grow
That's one thing I will never know
Still, I never had any stress
Which was fortunate I guess
For me the sun never shone
Will anyone remember me when I'm gone?
I only hope when I am laid to rest
People will know I did my best.

Frank Tonner

MEMORIES

As I reflect upon a life
Which saw me court, then take a wife
Our one and only son has grown
Moved out, and lives a life his own.

I used to think 'When I retire
I'll reminisce beside the fire'
Such pleasure's not for us today
For central heating's now the way.

And yet perhaps 'tis not so bad . . .
No humping coal, we should be glad.
Yet reminisce means looking back
We bought that coal . . . a bob-a-sack!

The times were hard but true to form
That single fire kept *us* warm.
It gave a cheery focal point
Boiled bath water . . . cooked the joint.

The simple pleasure I miss most?
A slice of 'open fire' toast.
No thoughts of 'will it help or harm?'
Spread thick salt butter from the farm.

Those days, this practice gave me bounce . . .
Today the *thought* adds one more ounce.
But, sat here in my 'central heat'
I'm now relaxed from head to feet.

Alan Isaac

THE WIND IN THE WHEAT

The wind in the wheat struck a sombre chord:
I imagined I saw the invading horde
As I saw them then, when the world was aflame.
Out of the sunrise, frenzied they came.

Mad dreams of conquest could not be denied,
Nations succumbed to the merciless tide
While the weak were abandoned to suffer and die.
Then came retribution, out of the sky.

And now is the reckoning, wave after wave
Eddying mindlessly, each one a slave
To the whim of the wind, which gathers apace,
And realisation transforms every face
To a mask of despair, unavailing they writhe;
For they, like the wheat, are awaiting the scythe.

J C Fearnley

SPIDERS

Spiders, the very word conjures up fear,
I run away when one comes near.
My sister's not scared, they cause her no fright,
If there's one in my room, I keep on the light.

They cling to the ceiling, watching me,
And dangle from threads which I can't see.
I don't know why I hate them so much,
It could be their wriggly, tickly touch.

It's worse when they come up the pipe to the bath,
They sit there and have a jolly good laugh.
I'm sure they know I'm really scared,
But next time I see one, I'll be prepared!

Claire Taskis

GHOSTS

They look down from their wall at me,
Apparelled in their finery;
    With frozen stare
    They're looking down,
    In shades of grey
    And shades of brown;
Always they glare censoriously,
No hint of who they used to be.

And yet I feel I know them well,
A whisper's breadth from me they dwell;
    They're all around,
    They guard, they guide,
    They gladden me,
    For by my side
All my forebodings they dispel,
They'd reach and grasp me if I fell.

And sometimes I, but dare I say,
Detect a lavender bouquet,
    And camphor oil
    Pervades the air,
    And smoking pipe
    Floats everywhere;
Could it be all the ghosts at play,
In shades of brown and shades of grey?

Hilary J Cairns

OUR FRIENDLY COMPUTER

My wife and I were happy, we lived a happy life!
We had no complications, no problems and no strife!
Then one day we decided, to keep up with the rest,
We'd buy a nice computer, with keys that could be pressed!

We went down to a showroom, to see what we could find;
And there a friendly salesman, so helpful and refined,
Was ready to assist us, with wise and good advice,
He said we'd need a printer and scanner at a price!

We'd also need a keyboard, a monitor and mouse;
And obviously a modem and a PC for the house!
He really was so helpful and sold us 'back-up' too!
We'd really have no trouble - his guarantee was true!

So, back home with our boxes, which on the floor we stacked;
We read through our instructions, before we got unpacked!
And soon, we had connected - the mass of tricky plugs,
Into the PC's sockets, with many puzzled shrugs!

At last, came our big moment! Our patience held in check,
We switched on our computer; with nerves - we were a wreck!
But such a lovely picture, appeared upon our screen,
We really had to marvel, at the things which could be seen!

We gazed in awe at 'Windows', our 'Desktop' was supreme,
Our 'Settings' were delightful, our 'Wordpad' was a scream!
We played and played for hours, so difficult to stop!
Alongside our computer, all else just seemed *a flop!*

We loaded it with 'software', with programmes - it was full!
We loved our dear computer, it was our favourite tool!
And then one day - disaster! Our life before us flashed!
And now we live in sorrow - for our computer 'crashed!'

R Bissett

THE CALL

The bird call blends - blessed thing -
the purest harbinger of spring -
with green abundance through the tree
and yet no songster do I see.

Thought is wasted - so much squander;
sour grievance wanes, tends to wander
away to one exquisite bar;
such notes - who knows where angels are?

Sequestered sequin of a song,
fragile, to whom does it belong?
Who graces Earth with such delight?
What utter bliss evades my sight!

The very absence of a bird
persuades me that the message heard
emanates from spiritual heights,
such flame of passion it ignites.

No actual libretto links
this operatic piece God thinks
to launch, surmounting leaves of jade
with what mere homo sapiens made.

I just feel honoured, singled out
to rise above rebuff and doubt;
perhaps I should accept such awe,
revere it though no bird I saw.

Ruth Daviat

POETRY IN MOTION

It's poetry time once again
So I will compose a short refrain
One that I hope will give lots of pleasure
One that I will always treasure.

So I just let my pen take hold
To write these words out big and bold
Hoping they will be read, far and wide
Filling me up with tremendous pride!

Barbara Coward

LONG SUMMER DAYS

When I was a child I loved to spend
Long summer days, without no end
Two weeks away on the Isle of Wight
To see the sea, was such a sight, the
Blue, blue sky with the sun above
We were as happy as turtle doves.
To buy the beach ball and the bucket and spade
To the seaside shop, a journey was made
To paddle and find the shells in the sand
With sweets from the shop in your hand.
Making sandcastles and a dip in the ocean
The countryside was poetry in motion.
The bubbly balls and the man on the prom
We tried to catch but they were gone
Before you could fill your net.
The ice cream cones, no mobile phones
It haunts my memory yet!
The theatre had plays, ah those were the days
Of laughter and gladness of sound.
Sometimes variety of shows notoriety?
Oh no! Arthur Askey was found.
A showman of laughter, remembered ever after
His song of the 'Bee', so profound.
The days were idyllic, the old fashioned village
Has altered but may still be found.
In blouses and shorts, you were taught
To run, on the edge, in the sea and
Splash along, while singing a song
To splash everyone with glee
A very long time no see!

Rosemary Peach

THE GHOST OF AN ADDICTION

Long, long ago it was I died, and yet I still recall
a velvet joy, delicious lust, to which I fell in thrall . . .

All sensuousness that will not die; the tastes of salt and sweat;
the scent of fluids fresh and sweet on bodies warm and wet . . .

Voluptuousness, all scarlet-silked, I grieved for in my grave;
it roused me from my slumberings, and I became its slave.

Each night I rise and walk the earth to seek a human bed;
and deep I drink from human love to keep me from the dead.

Each night I feed on passion's heat; each day I lie alone -
surrounded by the frigid earth, sour wood, and cold gravestone.

Desire shall keep my psyche warm - my earthbound soul from heaven;
for while I wait to love each night, my soul remains - unshriven.

I'd rather share a human bed, clasp close a human man,
and couple with him in his dreams, than lie with worms and sand . . .

Though long ago I turned to dust, the heat, my need, still lives;
I only pray God understands, and slaves to Love forgives . . .

Jenny Proom

GNOME FROM HOME

Why keep up with the Jones's?
The Jones's are utter pests,
Old Myfanwy, she never relaxes,
Old Ianto, he never rests.

Why keep up with Jones's?
They're always at Do It All,
Buying more gnomes for the garden,
And buying huge rugs for the hall.

Why keep up with the Jones's?
They've bought little Blodwyn a teddy,
That bear won't be lonely I wager,
Little Blodwyn has 20 already!

Why keep up with the Jones's?
They're always a step ahead,
They're having a *second* Jacuzzi,
They've ordered a six-poster bed!

If you're keen to keep up with the Jones's
There is no need to panic or fuss,
For I've just overheard the Jones's,
And *they're* trying to keep us with *us!*

Peter Davies

POETRY - (A LOVE OF)

I asked of words to be mine,
That I might share with them, their company,
Like that of the sunshine,
Whence out from its hiding place, behind the clouds,
Strode the pen,
- To give a helping hand -
That all others might then appreciate them.

Speech joined with verse,
In a chorus of song,
Rhyme too, having been invited to the party,
Decided, to come along.

And within the covers of an ever-open book,
The past and present, as the forward of the future,
Will forever survive,
For all who own within their lives,
The gift of poetry, as one of their loves.

Bakewell Burt

A COTSWOLD AUTUMN

The swallows have all flown
And leaves are turning brown.
In the garden down below
Dahlias bloom and glow,
And over the old stone wall
The ripening apples fall.

Soaring and swooping low
White wings follow the plough,
As the harvest fields are turned
After the stubble's burned,
And the ancient beeches stand
Watching over the land.

Under the glowing skies
The Severn Valley lies,
Distant hills a smudge of blue,
Silver river flowing through.
And sunset's orange flame
Fades as evening comes again.

Elizabeth Z Fennell

AUTUMN

A hazy sun shines from above
A morning misty, crisp and cold
The leaves float down to the ground below
A carpet of orange, brown and gold
That goes crunch, crunch, crunch beneath our feet
As on our way we go
Upon the fields flocks of birds gather to feed
Woodpigeons, gulls, rooks and crows
Squirrels scamper about on the ground
Searching for winter stores
Rushing here and rushing there
Hiding nuts galore
As winter approaches the nights will draw in
The weather will become colder still
The trees will stand naked, stripped of their leaves
In the midst of winter's chill.

Vanessa Bell

TO THE RHYTHM OF THE WHEELS

I am going on a journey through a flat and lonely plain
To somewhere and to nowhere, from pleasure into pain.
The train wheels are a-rolling and the rhythm shakes along,
The whistle keeps on blowing and the sun is bright and strong.
And the message of the engine as it runs its course today
Is a welcome and a warning as I travel on my way.
Come and share the journey with me, let me take you to the past
Where change and chance may follow with memories fading fast.

Those far-off days these places were a moment'ry delight -
Perhaps that's why the passing years reveal a certain light.
Now the train it is a-running, smoothly, swifter than before
And the journey's end is coming, so far from Scarboro's shore.
The endless fields and houses as they flash before my eyes
May throw up briefest moments of wonder or surprise,
While known and unknown faces are one in company
And I hold my one-time home in view with strange antipathy.

But what now is the greeting as I stand on solid ground
To view the many changes, and feel more lost than found?
The pavements here are thronging with crowds unseen before,
Once congested roads rejoicing to be precincts with full store
Of myriad attractions, music, frolics, flowers and fun . . .
But somewhere in my reverie I sense my time is done.
I shall not pass this way again - the past's ingrained too deep:
I turn and board the train once more, and lose myself in sleep.

Patricia Batstone

IN DISGRACE

Fergus was an exemplary cat,
Most obedient and, more than that,
His grateful owners said that he
Had kept their cottage rodent-free.

In fact, he seemed the perfect pet,
So angelic, restrained and yet
His alter ego, long suppressed,
Was waiting to be manifest.

He fell from grace. His halo slipped,
And then by base sensations gripped,
He faced the devil deep within
Who taught him the delights of sin.

Strange forces he could not control
Made him shatter the Meissen bowl.
The Grecian vase that he upset
Was an antique, one of a set.

Then treasured items he espied,
Priceless heirlooms, a source of pride.
He pushed the first and with one blow
They fell like ninepins in a row.

Lladro statues and china rare,
Things he wouldn't normally dare
To touch, he now began to edge
Wilfully over the marble ledge.

An exquisite porcelain jar,
Ming Dynasty, an objet d'art,
He reduced to worthless debris,
Cracked like eggshells - a tragedy!

Then conscience - even cats have one -
Made him realise what he'd done.
But if punishment were to follow,
Let it keep until the morrow!

Celia G Thomas

AGE

My seeds I've sown
The hay I've mown
And spring has fled away
My summer spent now old and bent

But still I've this to say
I've had my youth
It is the truth for this I had to pay
It's autumn now,

The autumn leaves fall past the eaves
My hair is turning grey
When white as snow
My hair does grow

My winter has begun
As a boy life was a joy
In youth I had some fun
As a man my life I planned
So to retire, in ease

But old and bent my health all spent
Now I cough and wheeze
Winter's chills brings other ills
And a trembling to the knees.

B D Vissian

THE OTHER DAY

The other day I started to cry,
But there was no reason why,
It was just something I had seen
On a big wide screen.

A movie that at first made me sad,
When it had finished I was glad.
Because there was happiness in the end
About a lady whose heart did mend,
For at first she had lost her lover,
But now she is happy with another.

Sally Warren

KITCHEN BLUES

When I enter the kitchen I feel dismay,
With its pots and pans gleaming away,
China, cutlery neatly in place,
Cupboards and drawers, fill in the space.

Cookery cards, recipe books,
I thought they were here, to help us non-cooks,
Try as I may, I can't comprehend,
Instructions that tell you to open one end.

Stand in boiling water, they tell you to do,
Why do that? I wish I knew,
I did what it said, but burnt my feet,
So much pain, just to cook meat.

Grill, poach, steam or fry,
Chop, slice, grate I'll try,
An ounce of this, a pinch of that,
Add the flour, then the fat.

At last a solution, I have found,
Now I listen for the magical sound,
A knock at the door, a ring of the bell,
The end is in sight, to my kitchen hell.

Pizza, Chinese or an Indian meal,
Relief and happiness is what I feel,
I answer the door, with money to pay,
The delivery man's here with my *take-away!*

Susan May Downs

MAROONED

The sun wounded,
Seeps of dawn,
Honouring the triumph of day's delight,
For dusk shall scar,
Before the star and moon avenge the night,
And so confess,
That nature's caress,
Can prove the largest wound,
And so impress,
That such a dress,
Could leave the earth marooned.

Anthony John Ward

BOOKS

What good
The books
Piled
On the shelf?
You should
Bring them
Down,
Educate
Yourself.

What use
The books
Closed
On the chair?
You should
Open
Now,
Their knowledge
To share.

What worth
The books
Left
On the stall?
You should
Buy them
Soon,
Then study
Them all.

Angela Pritchard

SCOTLAND IS THE HOME

Scotland is the home of the thistle,
Hear the wind and rain whistle.
Scotland is the home of Robert the Bruce,
He turned his army loose.
Scotland is the home of Robbie Burns,
How to write poetry he had learnt.
Scotland is the home of the kilt that is tartan,
The Scottish wear them in Dumbarton.
Scotland is the home of the haggis that is good to eat,
The Scottish think it is 'alreet'.
Scotland is the home of pipes and drums,
'Scotland the Brave' someone hums.
Scotland is the home of the Hogmanay, where they sing
                                    'Auld Lang Syne',
Meaning 'For the sake of Old Father Time'.
And have their wee dram,
As everyone danced and sang.

Tina Rooney

A Meteorological Mix

Take a ray of sunshine
A pinch of morning dew
Sprinkle in some snowflakes
A drop of rain or two
Whisk it all together
The dry ingredients sift
Season it with weather
Blend and mix and lift
Set aside to cool and chill
Melt and beat the topping ice
Add some fog to fit the bill
Till it rises neat and nice
Garnish it with rainbow
A tasteful dainty dish
Keep it till the storms go
And serve it with a wish!

Norma Macarthur

THE CLOSE

The busy milkman calls, the children play
The close awakes to yet another day
Houses and lawns neatly set out here
Everything is very bright and clear.

Once this was a garden, planned by a mother
Brought into being in memory of another
Sent far away many years ago
Resting in a foreign land, killed how we do not know.

When you enjoy all these lovely things
Think of a boy who proudly wore his wings
Journeyed far from these homely shores
Just to protect my life and yours.

In that land so far away many sleep the years away
Thankful for their duty done, and here we know of only one.
May he rest in peace so tender, knowing that we all remember.
May we guard the new generation, now the hope of all the nation.

D Creasey

CARMINE ROSE

Down in the valley
Where the green grass grows
There you will find rows upon rows
Shrubs, untamed,
Growing wilder by the hour
And nectar for insects just getting sour.

Down in the valley
Where the green grass grows
All alone you will find a solitary rose
A beautiful flower of crimson red
But oh so sad
It's nearly dead.

J M Stoles

SELF-DESTRUCTION

Deep within the Universe, lies our homely blue sphere,
which has been handed a curse, that's why aliens don't
come here,
with a future that's uncertain, unending deforestation,
combined with acid rain, across each and every nation,
as the trees are felled, once tall, majestic and cherished,
'timber' the logger yelled, the splendid tree had now perished,
another forest died, polluted and poisoned air,
it makes me sad, oh how I cried, it's so unfair,
why we are destroying our earth, the only home we know,
Mother Nature decimated from the time of its birth,
since the world was new, and the pace was slow,
it won't be long till it's dead, the oceans will no longer be blue,
as world pollution rears its ugly head, animals no longer roam the land,
that people once tried to save, creatures once so proud and grand,
the planet now a lonely grave, no one gives a damn,
can't you tell, that's why animals are better than man,
welcome to earth, welcome to hell, toxins dumped in our rivers,
radiation despoils the atmosphere, cancerous cells destroy our livers,
Earth. It's a nice place here!

K Delaney

THE WONDERFUL WORLD OF HALF-LIFE

The sound of a shotgun rings through the air,
Gordon Freeman had better beware.

Army helicopters struggle to fly,
Evil recons are destined to die.

Our hero silently creeps round the corner,
Must find scientists, he's gotta warn 'em.

Then a heart-rendering moment before his eyes,
The terrified scientist falls and dies.

But there's no time to stand and stare,
In this cruel world peace is rare.

Black Mesa, Office Complex, Lambda Core,
Adrenaline levels continue to soar.

Venturing further into localities unknown,
How much longer till he gets home?

Gerrard Shaw (14)

NONSENSE

Befuddled, bemused, dazed and confused,
straightforward, logical minds are not amused.
By histrionical contemporary verse,
examples of which, I've written worse.

But madness in rhyme is most enjoyable,
for amusing oneself, it's certainly employable.
It passes the time, whiles away the hours,
becoming beautiful, like spring's garden flowers.

Meaning it does not need, just metre and rhythm,
I write an awful lot, and sometimes give 'em
To people who appreciate, my sense of humour,
knowing I write nonsense, to make life less gloomier.

This one was easy, taking just ten and one minute,
and if you don't like it, then why don't you bin it?
'Cos you're right, it just doesn't make sense,
but I have a talent, for creating nonsense.

Danny Coleman

ABERFAN
21 October 1966, Forever One

Fifteen was my age when I heard the news
At that time the NCB had no views
A man sat with a tear on his cheek
Not caring that he is feeling so weak
Pictures on the screen his emotions fed
For the people that lived now lying dead
One hundred and sixteen children who shone
Twenty-eight adults all with their lives gone
Aberfan was this place of sudden death
To this day most will forget their last breath
Recorded the names of those departed
In minds of those left a thought is imparted
        Towards the moment Aberfan lives changed
        What would have happened if they would have aged?

James G Treharne

LISTENING

He listened to her footfall
on the stairs each Friday night;
and to her loving whispers
in the park, beneath the light.
he listened to her laughing
as she smiled and said 'I will,'
and her singing in the garden
gave his heart a special thrill.

He listened to her crying
when the doctor broke the news
that her illness would be terminal;
and he heard that she'd refuse
to have the special treatment
to control the slow decay
And he listened to her gasping
as she slowly slipped away.

And now he hears her calling
in the wind that bends the trees;
in the gentle breeze that's blowing
through the beeches' burnished leaves.
In the bubbling brook that babbles
in the soft sweet-scented air;
and he knows that she is waiting
till he comes to join her there.

J S Mercer

IN MY MIND

Soft poetry verse
Sweet words that flow
My eyes can't hold
Nor feel their glow

Sweet music song
Soft words that rhyme
To hear no tune
This curse is mine

To sing an ode
A poem to read
I find no scale
I've tried indeed

But in my heart
Where love is strong
With pounding beat
There lives my song

Within my mind
Where words are rife
For me sweet poems
They come to life.

Gordon McDonald

HOCUS-POCUS

Try to concentrate and focus.

It's no good looking at the page
And banging down your fist with rage.

I thought the writing bug had bitten?
So just cool down and be a kitten
And get that flippin' first line written.

Now you've started, watch your rhyming
And don't be jerky with the timing,
Or up the wall you will be climbing
And a breakdown you'll be priming.

Thus so far it's rather boring,
When it should be up and soaring
Making readers smile, adoring.

So there it is and don't you know it,
How can you call yourself a poet?

Your mind is full of hocus-pocus!

Cavan Magner

MARKING TIME

Through mud and plough fraught pheasant escapes
raucous beaters that stark fields traipse.
Stern marksman follows. His gun gapes

randomly into rain-laden clouds
that glower over ovine crowds
wearing woolly coats, winter shrouds.

Then day takes courage and fights the night
sun bathes grass with nourishing light
shy dormouse awakes, eyes gleam bright.

Val Don

ROUND TO GOD

Went into the Round Church Bowmore
not had a service there before
surprised to find God inside door;

especially on such a nice day
with the sea splashing in the bay
the sun clearing out all the grey

yet coming out of the sermon
God's answer to Job - 'Jesus gone'
cross out losses - for us He won.

Robert D Shooter

SUMMER

Rhododendron bushes pink
Upon the red roses blue tits sing
Out came from hives, the bees with its stinks

Butterflies, blue, white, brown and grey
All over my buddleias
To be seen

Jay birds lead their youth to flight
While the black cat pressing in
Chasing baby jay birds on the wing

Oh! Allow every cell of my being to sing
Summer has arrived
What a heartfelt joy it brings!

Kim Lee

MESS

So they destroyed me
with thorns that bled,
At Jordan I lay on that cross till nearly dead

act out your fantasies
of ease and no harm,
Messiah rise from the dead, to touch the past

Herod, Pilot may mock with dread, but it's never too hard, never too
cold for me,
he said I'd betrayed you, that my heart was ice,
But I'm sad at the grief and sacrifice

Alison Carr

THE BATS

At night their wings wave
Above the cold graves
Of moon's furtive gaze

They flutter ahead
While we're still in bed
No fear of the dead

By a river cold as ice
Ready to come back to life
Watch them late at night

Guided by a candle light
To see the bats that play at night
Jetting in and out of sight

Rodger Moir

TRIPLET

It was a cold, chilly day
at the tiny house beside the bay.
The trees rustled and the wind whistled away
beside the sea that day.

The stormy sea sounded like thunder.
How the tiny house survived I wonder.
The birds fly away with a blunder,
will they ever come back to see me I wonder.

But now the sunny skies sounded so peaceful,
the lambs are in the fields so beautiful.
The fresh spring seas look doubtful,
but my little house is still wonderful.

Sarah Milligan (13)

A Greyhound's Prayer

Oh Lord I pray, that soon one day
I'll see a kindly face
Whose heart I'd steal, my pain to feel
and take me from this place

Please hear my plea and set me free
from a life spent all alone
The nights are cold, the bedding old
I'm almost skin and bone

I ask no more than to know for sure
that a loving home awaits
Where I can share a comfy chair
beyond these iron gates

My needs are few, a little will do
so much to ease my strife
And in return, my love will earn
the saviour of my life

Claire Rolfe

THE SOLDIER

The soldier walks over sloping hills
Blisters cover his open heels
His jacket and trousers are all torn
He lowers his head as he mourns
All his friends have long been shot
Lying dead, alas he's not.
Blood flows slowly from his wounds
And he knows he'll join them soon
He can walk no farther on
He'll be dead before too long
Weary head thunders to the ground
Blood stains the muddied earth around
His spirit departs, hit by a shell
And his soul is thrown into hell
For he has killed twenty or more
He looked, he aimed, the army's law
He was told by someone he must fight
He tried to resist with all his might
He watched his friends fall at his feet
The unseen enemy that he cannot beat
So remember that soldier whose life he did give
For without this war, he would have lived.

Ann Taplin

A Mother's Charms

My task has started with your birth,
Protecting you from life on earth.
I cast out my protection charms,
To keep you safe within my arms.
I am your prison, hide in me,
When you mature I'll set you free.
I am your castle, stay in my walls,
I'll protect you from your many falls.
I am your ship, so sail in me,
I'll take you through life's stormy sea.
I am your time, I'm always here,
Protecting you from all you fear.
I am your mother filled with love,
And still protect you from above.
I am your god, come unto me,
I spent my lifetime watching thee.
I am your dreams, deep in your mind,
Step through the light and you will find,
I am your grave, lie down and rest,
Protected by the very best.
And after death my loving son,
Lay back inside my womb as one.

Linda Catherine Hind

HARVEST MOUSE

Tiny little harvest mouse
In the hedgerows builds her house,
Climbing tall grassy stalk
Hiding, watching, as you walk,
She is very, very shy
Keeping still as you pass by
Tiny ears, hear every sound,
She's not often on the ground,
Hangs by her long tail
Nibbling corn as farmers flail,
See the buzzard flying high
A warning to her, this eerie cry,
Scrambles quietly on her way
Keeping hid, and far away,
The farmer's barn is the best place
Among the straw without a trace,
She makes her nest, means no harm
Stays the night keeping warm,
After all she's very small
Tiny field mouse loved by all.

J Naylor

WHERE HAVE YOU GONE?

Cherished mother, how I miss thee
My treasured angel, where can you be?
Each night I watch stars up above
Searching the skies, for I so need your love
For knowing you're not really far away
Helps me through each lonely day
I feel your presence when I'm alone
I smell your things about my home
Mom, your photographs are everywhere
Each one I treasure, they help me bear
You sad passing from the world, dearest Mom
It's breaking my heart, where have you gone?
It's not easy for me, yet people say
Those tearful memories, will pass one day
But how could they, no they'll never understand
The loss of you, my mother so grand
Such empty feelings, fester deep within me
And where you are, I so long to be
No one prepared me for such pain, how sad
Or made me realise how much I'd really, truly had
I pick up your photos, my trembling fingers trace
Across such wisdom, that was once your face
For deep in those eyes I can truly see
That pictured image, that has become me
You gave so much, yet asked for nothing my Mom
And now from me, your loving soul has gone
There are no books in any library to explain
The loss of a mother, that soul-wrenching pain
Thank God for poetry, it helps me express
Those overwhelming feelings, that are life and death.

Ann Hathaway

HEAVEN ON EARTH

The car sped through the empty roads
and blackest night before the morn
right through the valleys of North Wales
to reach the bridge in growing dawn . . .

'Cross Menai then turn left to gaze
as wonders of all nature thrills;
the dewy grass, the sparkling tide,
the hamlets climbing up the hills.

The mountain top where eagles dare,
the hillside sheep above the trees:
the cattle stir as called by man:
the wheat ears tremble in the breeze.

Then dam the Menai if you must;
use tidal race to wattage make;
build wind-spun arms to give us power
to meet our needs for human sake!

But do not build a Sizewell here
lest should a Chernobyl befall:
just leave this patch of heaven intact
to God and Nature and us all!

Owen Edwards

IN THE PINK

The ample hippopotamus
Is not what you'd call glamorous,
And never inconspicuous,
Even when submerged in mud.
But it would be ridiculous
To challenge the chief 'potamus,
Or ever think to make a fuss,
Even though some young male could.

In Africa, it is quite rare
To find a creature who will dare
To challenge the great hippo's stare,
Even when he wants your food.
When croc or lion finds the fare,
The beach master is first one there,
And till he's full, he will not share.
He is one impatient dude.

So just in case you should, by chance,
Be opposite a hippo's glance,
Don't scream and shout or sing and dance,
Instead, three top tips from me:
Avoid his tusks - each is a lance;
Let him have first sunbather's stance;
Find his favourite treat, in advance,
Ripe fruits from the Sausage Tree.

When he's well fed he will feel calm
Then you'll be safe from hippo harm,
And he might go to have some fun -
Sunbathing 'til pink, in the sun.

Margaret Finter

FOR MY 'IRONING LADY'

Each day I go to work my shirt
Is clean and crisp like new,
Depending on the day and mood
It's striped, or white, or blue.

You iron my shirts with such expert craft
And it takes you so little time
I slip one on - so comfortable
Sends me out feeling fine.

No trace of a crease, not a mark
On a hanger, then put away
For me to choose, to wear with pride
Thanks to your care today.

So, daughter dear, when you iron my shirts
And make them smart as new
When I'm congratulated on my appearance
I give the credit all to you.

Mike Jackson

THE QUEEN OF CATS

In the day she sits on the bed without a care,
But in the night she's out the door without a minute to spare.
Over the garden, under the hedge,
Onto the wall, balancing on the neighbour's window ledge.
Knock, knock, knock on the window, bang, bang, bang on the door,
Until her delicate paws are red and raw.
The cats from numbers 9, 10 and 11 came out of their homes,
And padded across the tiny stones.
The cats walked for miles,
With faces which looked like great big smiles.
A couple of alley cats appeared and sneered,
But when they saw the queen they bowed and disappeared.
The cats walked till midnight,
Until they saw a shimmering light,
They went through a path in the trees,
Where hundreds of cats bowed on their knees.
The queen climbed up to her stand,
Whilst she and her children were being fanned.
She made her speech and stepped down,
While her oldest son started to frown.
'You don't have to do this,' he said;
'Yes, Son, it is fitting now you are wed.'
The prince smiled down on the younger cat beside him,
With her looks, personality and charm he was sure to win
The hearts and the confidence of the nation,
Together they'd be a feline sensation!
The queen rose to make her announcement, then handed
Her son the crown made with daffodils banded
With buttercups. The prince rose up to his full height
And spoke to the crowd. He told them he'd use all his might
To rule as his mother before him. She was right,
In her views, her policies, her beliefs and more.

He'd try to rule as fairly as she, he was sure
He could count on their support, his upbringing had assured that
As she placed the crown on his head, up went the cheer -
'Hail, King Cat.'

Jenny Osgood

ATMOSPHERE AROUND US

As I enter this atmosphere,
I feel as if I'm going to disappear,
This cold and misty feeling,
Standing there freezing.

As I enter this atmosphere,
Not knowing the fear,
Feeling a little chill up my spine,
Could this be the end of the line?

As I enter this atmosphere,
I feel the warmth in my ear,
As I look ahead, I see paradise.
No place on earth could be so nice!

As I enter this atmosphere,
I feel the hotness in my hair,
I see the deep blue ocean,
As I feel the cool emotion.

As I step out of this atmosphere,
I gaze up at the sky and stare,
So many feelings that surround me,
So many atmospheres around me.

Humma Taj (13)

BOYS' SCHOOL

In the early hours of the morning
Still dark but bathed in pale moonlight
The ivy-clad buildings of the school
Were shrouded and barely in sight.

Everywhere was peaceful and quiet
All were asleep or seemed to be
Even the dormitory was silent
Boys sleeping as far as you could see.

It was only a short time later
A figure in pyjamas appeared
It was a small boy moving slowly
Grasping the handrail as if he feared.

His face in the moonlight was youthful
As he walked down the steps so steep
But the moonlight did not find his eyes
For they were closed, locked in sleep.

Slowly he traversed the quadrangle
As he had done several times before
Until he reached the main stairway
And started climbing to the top floor.

Terry Daley

WAITING

The telephone keeps ringing and in excitement I answer the call
But it never ever is him, and it's driving me right up the wall.
I try not to show disappointment that it's a friend who has given me
a bell,
'Cause there surely is no ointment that can stop me going through
this hell.

The thoughts that pass through my mind are astonishing to say the least,
If only he could find a minute to make all these weird ideas cease.
With every passing moment the wilder my imagination grows
But is there some atonement that I can make that will banish
these prose?

One moment I really hate him, the next I am close to tears.
Oh Lord, is it a sin to so blatantly expose all my fears.
I cannot say I am really in love, but he's someone I really do like.
Maybe he thinks that's not enough, and he's saying to me
'on your bike'!

But still my imagination keeps playing some terrible trick.
I keep seeing him having an operation, or lying at home very sick.
I can see him there on his deathbed, trying to get me a word,
Then I start using my head, all these thoughts are completely absurd.

He's probably off with some bimbo, who is tall, blonde and fair.
Just leaving me here in this limbo, it's obvious he just doesn't care.
But maybe there's a simple explanation, why he hasn't picked up
the phone.
Still that doesn't balm my frustration, he is simply not sleeping at home.

There really is no point in torturing myself in this way
Or pushing my nose out of joint because he hasn't called me today.
I will simply have to learn to curb my impetuosity
And take every day as it turns, repeating 'What will be will be!'

Ann-Marie Esiaka

THE ACCIDENT

Lying in my hospital bed
With a bandage around my head
Legs in plaster and on my hand
That is why I could not stand
I had fallen from a horse chestnut tree
Climbing it was stupid of me
The branch had broken and I fell
As I did, I let out a yell
I saw stars as I hit the ground
It seemed ages before I was found
A woman took me to hospital in her car
Fortunately for me it wasn't very far
When my mother saw me she had a fit
For I was wearing my new football kit
There was blood on the shorts and the shirt was torn
My mother stood there looking real forlorn
She couldn't forget the money she had spent
Was put by for next month's rent
Because she loved me she had spent it on me
And I had been stupid to climb that tree
I wanted some conkers to take to school
When I think of the outcome, I was a fool

Diana Daley

SUMMER'S HEAVEN

The dewdrops, twinkling with a bright sheen,
On the wild rose, falling in streamers green,
All creeping shrubs scattering nearby,
Very colourful of a thousand dyes,
Wave in the soft winds of summer's sighs.
Each plant and flower so bright,
Belong to mountain's heavenly sight.
Embalming in the cool sweet air,
Hawthorn and hazel trees mingle there.
As primrose pale and violet flower,
Found in each clifftop a shady tower,
The wanderer's eye could barely view,
The summer's heaven's delicious blue.

Elisabeth Dill Perrin

THE COUNTRY IN SPRING

Snowdrops are peeping through grass oh so green,
Lent lilies are blooming beside the clear stream,
Hedges are studded with celandine bright
While the shy violets hide out of sight.

The leaves are unfurling to clothe trees in green,
Lambs skipping joyously in fields are seen,
Birds are all nesting in hedges and trees,
And the clear trill of skylarks drift down on the breeze.

Horse chestnut candles show white 'gainst the sky,
Enjoy Nature's bounty as you pass by,
Beech trees stand tall over carpets of blue
Where bluebells fill woodlands, and hedges too.

The country in spring is a place of delight,
Wherever you look you see a grand sight,
All Nature celebrates the winter's end
With colour and music that happily blend.

Marie Morgan

SPIRIT OF THE NORTH ON TRACK

Come spirit subtle and controlled,
With smooth and quiet power,
Articulate, informative,
Financially competitive and,
Swifter by the hour.

Loud were the ones who came before,
Who starred in films and galas,
Breathing fire in their armour bright,
Bronte hauntings to millennium light,
Tracked by Timothy Taylors.

Kathleen Mary Scatchard

TODAY - IS FOREVER

Life is for living
  and for forgiving -
    now - for today!
    We all know the way
      and for what we should pray -
        now - for today!
        Let's start a beginning
          of loving and giving -
            now - for today!
            for that is Christ's way.
            Give a smile, as you say -
            good evening, good day -
          now - for today!
            New friends you'll be winning,
              in the rain you'll be singing,
                and with you it will stay.
                Nothing's new under the sun,
                the past can't be undone -
              try as we may!
              So while it shines,
                let us make hay
                  and let love hold sway.
                  Soon, maybe tomorrow,
                  we'll meet with some sorrow -
                but even this Jesus refines.
                So as each one of us strives
                  towards our home in the skies,
                    to then meet our Lord's eyes -
                      may we hear His also -
                      'Well done'.

Beatrice Wilson

RHYME AND RHYTHM

A   is for Abba with their 'Dancing Queen'
B   are the Beatles and their 'Yellow Submarine'
C   are the Carpenters with 'Close to You'
D   is Neil Diamond with his 'Song Sung Blue'
E   is Gloria Estefan and 'Anything for You'
F   is Aretha Franklin with 'Who's Zooming Who'
G   are Guns 'n' Roses and 'Sweet Child O' Mine'
H   is Whitney Houston singing 'One Moment in Time'
I   are INXS who really 'Need You Tonight'
J   is Michael Jackson with his song 'Black or White'
K   is Gladys Knight who 'Heard it Through the Grapevine'
L   is Cyndi Lauper with her 'Time After Time'
M   is Madonna who's 'Crazy For You'
N   is Olivia Newton John's 'Xanadu'
O   are the O'Jays who are 'On a Love Train'
P   is for Prince and his song 'Purple Rain'
Q   is for Queen who 'Want to Break Free'
R   is Lionel Ritchie with 'Say You, Say Me'
S   is Rod Stewart singing hit 'Maggie May'
T   are 10cc on their 'Dreadlock Holiday'
U   is for U2 on 'New Year's Day'
V   are the Village People at the 'YMCA'
W   are the Walker Bros with 'The Sun Ain't Gonna Shine'
X   is XTC their 'Senses Working Overtime'
Y   is Paul Young and 'Every Time You Go Away'
Z   is for Zoe's 'Sunshine on a Rainy Day'

Helen Elizabeth Rawlinson

ONE WET TEACHER

Our teacher fell in the swimming pool,
During our lesson today.
It gave us all a bit of a shock,
We didn't know what to say.

It wasn't really funny,
She wasn't dressed for a swim.
She still had all her clothes on,
She didn't mean to fall in.

While we were all in the water,
She'd been walking along the side,
Watching, and telling us what to do -
But then, she started to slide.

She fell in with a great big splash!
It was such a funny sight.
We didn't know whether to laugh or not,
I think it gave her a fright.

'Oh dear, are you alright, Miss?
Do you need any help getting out?'
'No, thank you, I can manage.'
At least she didn't shout.

Then she was back on the side again,
She looked about ten feet tall.
Dripping wet, she carried on teaching,
As though nothing had happened at all!

Sue Smith

I'LL PUT THE KETTLE ON FOR TEA

'Twas a cold wet and windy night
Bleak and chilly not a cheerful sight
Umbrellas covered screwed up faces
Each going to their different places

My head it ached I was so weary
My eyes were streaming red and bleary
Packets of hankies I'd used for my nose
I sneezed and shivered I had such a dose

I got to the train to find it was late
Another half hour I had to wait
I wished this day had never begun
Indeed I felt so terribly glum

Some time later at last I got home
I heard a ringing it was the phone
I answered and found it was my best friend
To hear her voice cheered me up no end

'I'm coming round' is what she said
And now the pain had gone from my head
The gloom I felt it all had gone
Now that my friend was coming along

A cheery face soon appeared
'You had the flu is what I feared
But now I see you're feeling better'
I blessed the day that I had met her

'I'll put the kettle on for tea'
These words they echoed joy to me
My recovery it was plain to see
Because the kettle was on for tea

Janet McBride

I'VE LOVED YOU FROM AFAR

I've loved you from afar,
I've tried to make you dear,
I've imagined you so often,
Your beauty, so very clear.

I've longed to make you mine,
I've held you in my dreams,
I've kissed your gentle lips,
Your golden hair that gleams.

I've lived my part and true,
I'm happy now you see,
I know you love me well,
I'm glad I set you free.

JSC Sutherland

ASTRONAUTS AND AIR BALLOONS

Astronauts and air balloons, Concorde and Titanic
Astrology and alcohol and everything Satanic
Microlights, motorbikes, the hermit and the wanderer
Scientists and psychopaths, the idiot and the blunderer.

Transgressors and oppressors, tiaras and tears
Transcendental meditation and phobias and fears
Criminals, kings, the wicked and the witch
Death awaits each one of us, destitute or rich.

Do you walk that narrow path towards that narrow gate
Do you know when time is set for you to meet your fate
Do you understand the truth that Jesus died for you
Do you believe God's Holy Word is infallible and true?

Almighty God so loved the world He sacrificed His Son
His crucifixion paid the price for what we all have done
The gift of eternal life is there for you to choose
Ultimately each individual decides to win or lose
Search your heart and you will find there is an empty space
It's waiting to be filled right up with His amazing grace.

Desiree Knoesen

THE RAINBOW

Thunder is the anger God feels about man,
They are still as selfish as when time began.
Rain poured down from a sullen sky,
Made from his tears as *He* asked himself why?
Dark clouds rolled up to hide from view,
Man's inhumanity, in the image of you.
Then I caught a glimpse of the sun,
'Is there still hope for everyone?'
Then magical, mystic colours appeared,
The future might not be as bad as we feared.
The rainbow I saw could land anywhere,
With a pot full of wonderful wisdom to share.
The colours will fade like me, growing old,
But the wisdom of God will always be told.

Milly Hatcher

I'LL LOVE YOU TILL THE END OF TIME

As the raindrops come down upon my face,
The wind blows coldly through my hair,
Hiding those tears of despair.
As I walk alone,
Thinking of this love untold.

Still I'll love you till the end of time.

As my body tingles from the cold,
My toes and fingers numb,
Like my heart they have lost all feeling, once more never healing.
Confused at what I've done,
Knowing that I have not won.

Still I'll love you till the end of time.

The moon gets dimmer like my heart,
Now my darling we're apart.
Lost and torn between a bush,
But I said it with a hush.
I really didn't mean to push.

Still I'll love you till the end of time.

I know my love you have to go - parting is not easy,
But words have been left unspoken,
For this love there is no token,
Not even when I've woken.
Just a person left heartbroken.

Still I'll love you till the end of time.

One day you'll see this love was meant to be,
But this could take until eternity.
I gave you my heart, it was yours to meet,
So my memories they will keep.
But you were the one who made me weep.

Still I'll love you till the end of time.

I thought you were mine to keep,
We shouldn't have taken that leap.
My love for you will never die,
But you were the one who told the lie.
This my love was not I.

Still I'll love you till the end of time.

But now I know of your lies and deceit,
No more will they make me weep,
Because now I am not as weak.
Now I've found the light so bright,
Shining upon me like a star.

Still I'll love you till the end of time.

Edith Wood

THE ADDICTIVE GARDEN CENTRE

Garden centre with shrubs and blooms,
For the garden and conservatory rooms,
Energetic intention to groom.

Spring 'tis a magical month,
Toil then relax for lunch,
Pebbles feet can crunch.

Man-made waterfall looking grand,
Ditch filled with sand,
Toddler bucket and spade in hand.

Clean swing and helter-skelter,
Lawnmower, service the motor,
Barbecue bricks and mortar.

Daisies appear on my lawn,
A dandelion looking forlorn,
Gee it's great to be born.

Patio with chairs and table,
Lemonade for Auntie Mabel,
Sunshade strong and stable.

Spring, summer, winter fades,
Purchasing gadgets all man-made
The garden centre again I invade.

Alice Harrison

THE SPLENDOUR OF ISLAY

There's an island I once knew
Where in childhood I grew
Memories keep coming back to me.
Oh, I know I'll be merry
As I journey on the ferry
When the splendour of Islay I will see.

When I was a boy
I played on the shore
Sometimes Port Ellen
Sometimes Bowmore.
Those years have long gone
A hundred years it seems
Since I left dear Islay
To follow my dreams.

I have travelled round the world
I have sailed the seven seas
But my heart has remained in the Hebrides.
Some day I'll come home,
Some day I'll make my way
Back home to dear Islay
No more will I stray.

I will wander o'er the hills
Take the road to Laggan Bay,
Meander through the heather
Cross the fields of hay.
I will wander round my island
Look up some old friends
For I must return to Islay
Before my life ends.

Hamish M Davidson

LOVE'S NOT

Love's not the pretty tablecloth
That's spread when lovers dine,
It's the flavour that they savour
In the food and in the wine:

It's not the showy serviettes,
The ornate serving bowl,
Just tasty food and drink that whets
The hungry cockles of the soul!

Love's not soft music, lights turned low,
Wax candles, works of art;
It's the warm and lambent flames that glow
In one another's heart:

Love's not the coffee, sipped to end
A hearty meal, together,
It's the precious gift you give a friend,
You want to keep forever.

Nicholas Winn

IS IT ME OR THEM?

I sat with pen poised, and as the clock chimed
Thought of all the old poets whose poetry rhymed
I bought a book of poems costing six pounds, ten pence
And not one of the poems just made any sense

Now don't misunderstand me, I am not a quibbler
I am only an old amateur scribbler
But to make my point, I sat down and took
Just one example from my over-priced book

(Quote)
'The flickering flame reflected the mood
of a tormented soul reined in by anguish of apathy'

Now how could that be submitted *and* expected to win
I simply recommend that (poet) to the loony bin

Time for rhyme must be quickly resurrected
And I submit my rubbish, as you suggested
In the forlorn hope that this poem meets
With the same consideration as Tennyson or Keats

Terry Guy

In The Geriatric Ward

Demented Dorrie, delicate and frail,
With sunken eyes and cheeks so gaunt and pale,
Propped on her starchy pillows, snowy-white,
A ghostly presence in the autumn light,

Seems quite unheedful of the restless sound
Of bustling nurses on the morning round,
The stern, efficient doctors as they fly
From bed to bed with hardened practised eye.

Sphinx-like, she sits and, vacantly, she stares,
As one who long has shuffled mortal cares,
And left the empty busyness behind,
A silent prisoner of a broken mind.

But when small Jo is lifted up to trace
With plump, smooth hand the furrows of her face,
And gently stroke a thinning, silver tress,
The child alone can see her loveliness.

Jackie Lapidge

NEGOTIATION

Life is a negotiation, an ongoing investigation,
revolved around presentation, in the aim to reach our destination,
involving much concentration, grit and determination
to do the best in any given situation,
full of much legislation, rules and stipulation opening us up to
vulnerability and temptation.
So find some inspiration using the imagination find the train at
life's station, except no imitation nor any form of manipulation,
expand on education, it may increase mental stimulation.
Make good of life's creation it could have some relation to
some form of realisation or even self actualisation.
Hopefully after reading this written illustration you will make some
demonstration of finding your own revelation.
Did I mention life is a negotiation.

Jay Pacer

FADS AND FASHIONS

Fashions come and fashions go
They hold our interest and so
We try them on, some will flatter
Some appal us for that matter

Skirts go long and then go shorter
We liked them long so should we alter?
Shall we go against the grain
And hope they'll soon come back again?

Colours also ring the changes
Shops are filled with these new ranges
So we buy them, it's like a game
Then wonder why we all look the same?

One Christmas thinking we would look the most
Dressed all in white, we looked like ghosts
When skirts went short, our legs we froze
Our maxi coats took care of those

High buttoned jackets for the men
Doubled breasted now and then
Trousers narrowed, trousers flared
Made for everyone who dared

Nipped in waists, shoulders higher
Things to tempt the shrewdest buyer
Hats are quite a different matter
They should fit and they should flatter

And what of shoes, to take us places
Some are slip-on, others laces
Shoes that sometimes make you think
To walk on those you'd need a drink

Hair piled high to frame a face
Sprayed to keep it in its place
Sometimes short, sometimes longer
Coloured pale or coloured stronger

Ever-changing optimisted
New, intriguing and artisted.

Mavis Rachel

WHAT IS THIS HOUR?

In winter when the sun is high
No stars to shine in the moonlit sky
When hymns are sung and lessons read
We still partake of wine and bread.

As lights are glowing from Christmas trees
And people on their bended knees
Are still remembering on this night
The truth of Christmas - in the quiet.

The bells that peal as people sing
And listen to the familiar ring
Of carols new and Scripture old
That speak of wonders long foretold

Yet in amongst the solemnity
Thoughts are wondering of that to be.
As Christmas day approaches soon
Are all the preparations done.

The children - are their stockings filled?
Has Santa been and gleefully willed?
That everyone a present should have
Just so like Jesus - who came to save.

What is there left of Christmas love
Of peace and joy sent from above?
For us we all so humbly pray
Is the truth in us all today.

The birth that happened long ago
Filled the air with heavenly glow
If only it could be the same
The whole world over - yet again.

This hour at midnight
In pure delight
People flock to churches bright
To sing out loud
With voices proud
In amid a familiar crowd
Their hearts are light
Smiling bright
At this wonderful hour of midnight.

Janet Collinson

INSTRUCTIONS TO MADNESS

Hammer home a brighter cork
Sing for me your glory walk,
Give no answer to sad tales
Reap rewards of slower snails.

Shine genius on a melted page
Lie with ease, increase the rage
Put up signs that call nine clouds
Hint for sun to rip targets loud.

Frown a day so you can start
Never leave untyped a paper heart,
Make sense of none to crush a pill
Finish freedom flowing stronger still.

Come softly to forward backways
Bleed snowfall, hear the taunt of daze
Breath and blister reality, make a tune
Read your lifeline, hand to the moon.

Cut down sins you have bent
Retreat in front of love coins spent,
Wake orange fields with loud silence
Keep hold the rope, faking guidance.

Come out of nowhere raining ink
Space out losing with golden drink,
Take my advise and stroll the same shelf
Deal cards foreign distant, look in from out yourself . . .

Victoria Jukes

THE SANDS OF TIME

The sands of time are passing
And we are older grown,
Can we look back with gladness,
At the seeds that we have sown?
Or do we look in sorrow,
At some of the things we've done,
We've caused another's heartache
By something said in fun.

As we look back on our teenage years
The years of love and laughter,
And the one we loved who left us lone,
The pain and sorrow after,
Can we forgive and love again
This time perhaps forever.
To pledge our love and keep it
In a bond that none can sever.

We must look forward, never back
As we go our chosen way
The sands of time are passing
Slowly every day.
Don't let them pass you by, my friend
Make use of every day.
To spread a little kindness
In all you do and say.

To make the world a happier place,
And bring a smile to someone's face.

Isobel Laffin

SKIES ADJOURNING

An opened sky of glossy blue,
O view the transient hue,
Kiss to the face joy anew,

Sing as ye oceans atoll,
Alas boldly our souls go . . .
A view of blue I stole,

Beheld in our minds so dear,
The waves of long-lost drear
Of adverse sorrows were near,

Faint then methinks the crime,
Heavens doom the soul of mine,
Warring wild is life divine,

Sight the storm upon the bowers
Charading haunts of flowers,
A harmony of worldly empowers,

Day by day the patronage,
By what slight the privilege?
The false world disengaged,

Heed then I went a-heleboring,
And hopeless was the mourning,
So skies have gone adjourning!

Linda Curtis

FAREWELL, MILLENNIUM

Ebbing life, Millennium's corpus lay,
recalling times, this final day,
limited by pulse and tears
to thoughts of these last hundred years.

Flashed on retinas of mind,
Mafeking its earliest find;
'Frisco's' quake set town to flame;
suffragettes in social claim.

Conquered was the Southern Pole!
In tragedy, Titanic's role.
The first World War, the blood it cost:
forty million lives were lost!

Racing now cross mental screen,
numerous pictures, briefly seen:
Hitler's war; our gallant Few;
the Holocaust; that bomb, we knew.

Now Armstrong bounces on the moon:
Sinatra's voice; the women swoon!
The century dies . . . the pictures haze . . .
as fireworks set the Thames ablaze!

Ron Hails

DO YOU FEEL GOOD?

Don't you feel good
When you help someone in need?
Knowing you have just done a great deed

Don't you feel good?
When you make someone happy
Knowing you have just cheered someone up

Don't you feel good
When you try your best at school?
Knowing you have just improved your future

Don't you feel good
When you give money to a charity?
Knowing you could have saved a life

Don't you feel good
About yourself, the way you look
About your health?

When you feel bad
Think about why
Don't ever feel bad. No need to cry.

Kirstie Hall (14)

TO ALL NATURE

I mused once on a blooming rhododendron tree
Its blossom so beautiful that any would hearten to see,
And as I spared some moments in its sight
And evening drew on - its petals cool
Would fall - and falling would
Appreciate all before and fallen lost already.
Spring hardly started - but nature's steady hand
Will take away some of which it gives.
It is how the natural world survives
And we should not be afraid or draw away
For Nature is magnificent in all its story.
On looking in the world's garden
(The world of nature that comes to the fore it seems
In Springtime)
The message is;
A lesson to be learned.
Our thoughts are by nature turned
And we are in its thrall.
The exquisiteness of its beauty shows
That there is more to the world
Than mere thought could or heaven dream of.
The world in that moment is unfurled,
Its beauty rarely shown in its completeness
Our cup overflows
We must just be so grateful.

C J Bayless

LITTLE MOMENTS

Ribbons, bows
babygro's
tiny shoes
socks too

bottles, dummies
full time mummies
sons, daughters
baby walkers

Christmas mornings
as day is dawning
frolics in snow
hot cocoa

sandy beach
a castle each
fun fairs
teddy bears

so long ago
how they grow

boyfriends
girlfriends

working lives
husbands, wives

well you never know
grandsons, daughters

mitten knitters
baby sitters.

James Reid

RELAXING IN THE TWILIGHT HOUR

How lovely in these days of stress and strife,
To leave behind all the problems of modern life,
The rumbling of rushing traffic in busy street,
As we hurry along on tired and aching feet.

To relax in time between day and night,
The witching hour, known as twilight,
The harshness of nature with beauty endowed,
All forms appearing in a mystic shroud.

In country lane, traffic hum a distant sound,
Where scented hedge blossom and wildflower abound,
Damp spiders' webs, all glistening white,
Show their delicate tracery in the misty twilight

Silhouette of buildings in the fading light,
Soon to vanish with the coming of night,
Stark outline of a lightning struck tree,
A giant figure in torment, struggling to be free.

How kind to the vision is this time of day,
Giving everything a look, transient and fey,
This bewitching time in the twilight hour
Revives the tired spirit, like rain to a flower.

E Kathleen Jones

MAKE THE WORLD LESS BLUE

Two thousand years ago, they say,
Christ was born on Christmas day.
To bring hope of love and joy and peace,
All hate and war, hence forth should cease.
Why did that all go astray?
Did greed and fear get in the way?
Put away the things of war,
Let Heaven and Earth be built once more.
Come on, brothers, sisters too,
Let's make the world far less blue,
And the new Millennium
Be full of happiness and fun
For everyone.

R Champion

THE ROSE-COLOURED STARLING OF TWITCHERS' CLOSE

Ramblin' Rose, Ramblin' Rose,
A fugitive from Asian snows
Pitches at Hanham to warm his toes
And when he finds he's quite unfroze
He decides to stay and have a moze.
So following his eyes and then his nose,
He sees a place where the lady throws
Food for the birds where her garden grows.

Soon the net gets hot and the birdline glows
With news of the starling coloured rose
Who's settled at Hanham, the place he chose
To feed his face and warm his toes
Until sufficiently adipose.
From North, South, East and West arose
Twitcher on twitcher in serried rows
In the road they've renamed 'Twitchers' Close'.
Is that sturnus roseas do you suppose?
Perched on that chimney to warm his toes
Or on top that tree in his winter clothes.

So the word gets round and the story grows,
The excitement mounts and the next he knows
He's caught on camera for a TV pose.
Now the experts discuss the cons and pros
Whether he'll stay till winter's close.
But I'll tell you what any bird brain knows
That it's better to stay and warm your toes
Where your bread's buttered and your heart glows
Than winter in the land of Asian snows.

So look out for the sign in 'Twitchers' Close':
'Rose-coloured starling - mon repos'.

Brian Iles

Untitled

In the north of Wales are the Swallow Falls
and many other waterfalls.
They cascade down lush mountainsides,
sparkling and tinkling as my memory recalls.

The little trains of Wales,
chug up the mountainside.
One romantic journey ends
at the beautiful Tallillyn lakeside.

Sandy beaches, pretty bays,
surround the coast of Wales.
From north to south the valleys run,
their beauty never fails.

The beauty of this little land
is reflected in the people.
Tragedy has often come from many, many sources,
but the land is dotted everywhere with tiny chapel steeples.

For Wales took Jesus to their hearts
again and again over time.
They express their love in music and song,
the valleys and hills ring with music sublime.

Like people the whole world over
who've known real tragedy.
The people of Wales *know* the suffering servant,
His love and beauty sets their hearts free!

Their lilting speech and welcoming smiles
are generously spilled out.
Though other faiths have entered into the rest of the British Isles,
in Wales 'Jesus' is the victory shout.

So if you long for peace and rest,
treat yourself to a visit to this land of music and song.

Margi Hughes